Macarons Cookbook for Beginners

Prepare the Best Macaroons in Different Flavors and Colors

BY: Allie

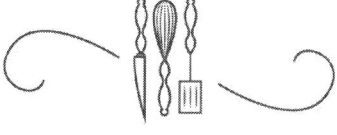

COOK & ENJOY

Copyright Notes

This book is written as an informational tool. While the author has taken every precaution to ensure the accuracy of the information provided therein, the reader is warned that they assume all risk when following the content. The author will not be held responsible for any damages that may occur as a result of the readers' actions.

The author does not give permission to reproduce this book in any form, including but not limited to: print, social media posts, electronic copies or photocopies, unless permission is expressly given in writing.

Table of Contents

Easy and Delicious Macaron Recipes

ssssssssssssssssssssssssssssssssssssssssssssssss

1) Basic French Macarons

This is the basic French Macaron recipe to which you can add different flavors, fillings and create as many types of macarons you want. All macarons have this recipe as the base so we thought of sharing it first after which we will show you how to can add different tastes to it.

Cooking Time: 120 Min

Makes: 20-25

List of Ingredients:

- ¼ cup of white sugar
- 1 cup of finely ground almonds
- 1 2/3 cups of any confectioners' sugar
- 1 - teaspoons of vanilla extract
- 3 egg whites

ssssssssssssssssssssssssssssssssssssssssssssssssssssss

Procedure:

Line your baking sheet with a silicon baking mat.

Beat the whites in a bowl with a whisker until peaks are formed. Then add in the sugar and extract until eggs are glossy. Mix the confectioners' sugar and the almonds in a separate bowl first and then fold them into the egg mixture.

Now take a piping bag and add the batter into it and make like 3-4 cm of circles on your baking sheet. Let it rest for 15-20 minutes so the better can be flat and rested. The disks should be apart from one another so they can be baked easily. Once you have made all your circles with the diameter leave it outside for an hour until the top gets a hard skin.

Now pre-heat your oven at 140 degree C.

Bake the cookies for around 10-15 minutes and cool them off.

Fill with any of your favorite fillings and enjoy the macarons.

2) Strawberry Macarons

Strawberries are fresh, sweet and sour and just perfect for anything. So today we decided to make these perfect things a bit better by incorporating them into macarons. Yes, strawberries and macarons, the perfect combination for any special event! Is there anything more you can ask for?

Cooking Time: 120 Min

Makes: 30

List of Ingredients:

- 212g of Almond Meal
- ¼ cup of Pureed Strawberries
- 82g of Egg Whites
- 212g of Confectioners' Sugar
- 90f of Egg Whites, Divided
- 158g of Water
- 236g of Sugar
- 1 cup of Unsalted Butter
- A Pinch of Salt
- 2 cups of Confectioners' Sugar
- 1 teaspoon of Pure Vanilla Extract

ssssssssssssssssssssssssssssssssssssssssssssssssssss

Procedure:

Make the batter of the French macarons; add a little red food color if you like just to complement the strawberry macaron recipe.

Bake these macarons and let them cool down.

Now take the butter and cream with the help of a whisker until it's fluffy.

Then add in the confectioners' sugar and salt until all of the sugar is incorporated and it results in a fluffy mixture.

Now add in the vanilla and pureed strawberries and mix until it becomes a thick creamy mixture.

Keep the mixture in a fridge to cool it down and then fill in the macarons.

3) Almond Joy Macarons

Again a recipe for the nut-fans out there! Stick to your basic coconut macaron recipe but just add on some almonds for that extra crunchy taste. You can replace almonds with any other nuts of your choice. This is the beauty of these recipes that once you get to know them, you can start making your very own.

Cooking Time: 30 Min

Makes: 10

List of Ingredients:

- 2 tbs. of all-purpose flour
- 1/3 cup of sugar
- 1/8 - teaspoons od salt
- ½ cup of large almonds
- 2 egg whites
- 4 ounces of melted dark chocolate
- 1 cup of flaked coconut
- ½ teaspoon of vanilla extract

sssssssssssssssssssssssssssssssssssssssssssssssssssssss

Procedure:

Take a bowl and mix the sugar, coconut, salt, eggs, vanilla, cranberries and flour and stir everything well.

Drop small rounded balls on a lined sheet and press one almond on top of each and bake for around 15-20 minutes in a pre-heated oven at 325F.

Drizzle the melted chocolate on top before serving.

4) Coffee Macarons

Till now you must have be an expert in making French macarons so now play with some new flavors. We all love coffee and a lot of people prefer desserts of coffee flavor and this coffee based macaron can be enjoyed at breakfast or tea time. The taste is incredible!

Cooking Time: 120 Min

Makes: 20

List of Ingredients:

- 110g of almond flour
- 200g of powdered sugar
- ¾ teaspoon of instant espresso powder
- 1 teaspoon of vanilla extract
- 3 egg whites
- 25g of granulated sugar
- ½ cup powdered sugar
- 4 tablespoons of softened unsalted butter
- 1 tablespoon of coffee liqueur

ssssssssssssssssssssssssssssssssssssssssssssssssssss

Procedure:

Pulse the powdered sugar, almond flour and espresso in a processor until it's combined.

Now whip the egg whites and vanilla in a foamy mixture separately.

Add up the granulated sugar and beat until you get a glossy meringue.

Fold in the almond mix to these whipped eggs well.

Now pipe this mixture into small diameters on a lined baking tray.

Keep them at room temperature for an hour so the top becomes stiff.

Bake the macarons for 15-20 minutes in a pre-heated oven at 280 degrees F.

Now for the filling beat the powdered sugar, unsalted butter and liqueur until you get a creamy mixture.

Fill in the cooled macarons and enjoy.

5) Coconut Macarons

As a coconut lover, we have tried multiple recipes of coconut macarons. These turned out to be our most favorite as they are the simplest ones and taste amazing. Chewy and moist on the inside and golden crispy on the outside, what more can you ask for?

Cooking Time: 30 Min

Makes: 10

List of Ingredients:

- 2 tbs. of all-purpose flour
- 1/3 cup of sugar
- 1/8 - teaspoons OD salt
- ½ teaspoon of vanilla extract
- 2 egg whites
- 1 cup of flaked coconut

sssssssssssssssssssssssssssssssssssssssssssssssssssss

Procedure:

Take a bowl and mix the sugar, coconut, salt, eggs, vanilla and flour and stir everything well.

Drop small rounded balls on a lined sheet and bake for around 15-20 minutes.

6) Rose Macarons

Rose macarons are quite popular among females also. They taste amazing together and look great at any tea party. The rose water taste is not over-powering, just enough to give it a slight taste which makes them perfect.

Cooking Time: 120 Min

Makes: 20-25

List of Ingredients:

- 3 large egg whites
- 150g of icing sugar
- A few drops of rose water
- Pink food coloring
- 75g granulated sugar
- 1 - teaspoons of rose water
- 100g of ground almonds
- Around ¼ - teaspoons of pink food coloring
- 90g of butter
- 175g icing sugar

ssssssssssssssssssssssssssssssssssssssssssssssssssss

Procedure:

Add the sugar and ground almonds in a processor and whizz for around 30 seconds and then sift the mixture in a bowl.

Now whisk the egg whites in a large bowl until you get soft peaks. Drop in the sugar in 3 batches and whisk along to create glossy meringue.

Now add half of the almond sugar mixture with coloring and rose water. Fold with a spatula for a minute.

Spoon your mixture in a piping bag and pipe circles around 4cm in diameter on your lined baking tray. Leave it for 30 minutes or so for the mixture to settle before you hit the oven.

Set your oven to 190 C and bake the macarons for 10 minutes until they are crispy. Take the tray out and let them cool.

Now for the filling, soften the butter and beat the sugar, rose water, water and food coloring to make a bright pink mixture. Now pipe one base of the macaron and sandwich it with another one and serve.

7) White Chocolate Cranberry Coconut Macarons

We just can never have enough dry fruits and chocolates in our recipes and we hope so is the case with most of you out there. So this recipe is made with adding on some tasty dried cranberries and pure white chocolate. It's the best any dessert can get and we assure you one will never be enough for your taste buds.

Cooking Time: 30 Min

Makes: 10

List of Ingredients:

- 2 tbs. of all-purpose flour
- 1/3 cup of sugar
- 1/8 - teaspoons od salt
- ¾ cup of dried cranberries
- 2 egg whites
- 4 ounces of melted white chocolate
- 1 cup of flaked coconut
- ½ teaspoon of vanilla extract

ss

Procedure:

Take a bowl and mix the sugar, coconut, salt, eggs, vanilla, cranberries and flour and stir everything well.

Drop small rounded balls on a lined sheet and bake for around 15-20 minutes in a pre-heated oven at 325F.

Drizzle the melted chocolate on top before serving.

8) Pistachio Macaron

Pistachios are the tastiest nuts of all and this is the reason why pistachio macarons are amazing too. The green color not only looks great but leaves you wanting more. The recipe is really simple and easy but will dirty up a lot of dishes but the reward in the end is worth everything.

Cooking Time: 120 Min

Makes: 20-25

List of Ingredients:

- ¼ cup granulated sugar
- Half cup of raw pistachios
- 2 tablespoons of almond flour
- ¼ cup almond paste
- 1 tablespoon of vegetable oil
- ¼ teaspoon of almond extract
- ¼ cup of unsalted butter
- 4-5 drops of green food coloring

ssssssssssssssssssssssssssssssssssssssssssssssssssss

Procedure:

Following the basic French macaron recipe, add in the green coloring and bake your cooking like before.

Now let's come to the pistachio filling.

First take a saucepan and add the sugar and some water and bring it to boil. Cook the syrup until it reaches 250 degrees F.

Now add in the toasted pistachios and stir until all of them are coated with the sugar. Take them out and let it cool.

Now place the pistachios in a food processor with the almond flour and blend until the mixture becomes coarse. Slowly add in the oil to blend, add the butter, almond paste and 3 tbs. of water and continue mixing until a paste is formed.

Then fill your baked macarons with this filling once they are cooled.

9) Funfetti Coconut Macarons

Till now you must be aware of the many types of coconut macaron recipes. But don't they all seem plain and simple? What to do when you want to make those macarons for a fun party? You jazz up those macarons and this recipe will show you how! It's equally simple and colorful.

Cooking Time: 30 Min

Makes: 10

List of Ingredients:

- 2 tbs. of all-purpose flour
- 1/3 cup of sugar
- 1/8 - teaspoons od salt
- 1 pack of colorful edible confetti
- 2 egg whites
- 1 cup of flaked coconut
- ½ teaspoon of vanilla extract

sssssssssssssssssssssssssssssssssssssssssssssssssss

Procedure:

Take a bowl and mix the sugar, coconut, salt, eggs, vanilla, confetti and flour and stir everything well.

Drop small rounded balls on a lined sheet and bake for around 15-20 minutes in a pre-heated oven at 325F.

10) Salted Caramel Macaron

Why would you want to go for normal caramel when you have salted ones to do favors to your taste buds? The salt and sweet balance in this recipe is amazing. If you haven't tried out salted caramel before then we highly recommend this recipe to you.

Cooking Time: 120 Min

Makes: 20-25

List of Ingredients:

- 250g of heavy cream
- 10g fleur de sel
- 350g castor sugar
- 350g of butter cut into small cubes

sssssssssssssssssssssssssssssssssssssssssssssssssss

Procedure:

First place the cream into a small saucepan and cook until it starts to boil.

Take another saucepan and pour in the sugar and stir it so it starts to caramelize. Once it reaches the dark color, remove from heat and add in the sugar and stir with a spatula.

Let it cool down a bit and then add the fleur de sel and the butter and continuously mix it. Once all the butter has been mixed thoroughly pour the caramel in a container and let it cool in a fridge.

Once cooled beat it until it reaches a fine and shiny texture.

Make the basic French macarons and fill them in with this creamy filling.

11) Chocolate Dipped Coconut Macarons

Like coconut but still want a chocolate taste to it? At the same time you're huge fan of macarons? Then this recipe is the answer to all of your sweet desires. It's a pretty simple take on the regular coconut macaron recipe with a little twist of chocolate which is not too much but enough to satisfy the cravings.

Cooking Time: 125 Min

Makes: 10

List of Ingredients:

- 4 large egg whites
- 1 14-ounce package shredded coconut (sweetened)
- 2/3 cups of sugar
- ¼ teaspoon of kosher salt
- 1/3 cup of flour (all-purpose)
- 6 ounces of bittersweet or semisweet chocolate
- ½ teaspoon of vanilla extract (pure)

sssssssssssssssssssssssssssssssssssssssssssssssssssss

Procedure:

Heat your oven to 325F.

In a bowl, mix the coconut, flour, sugar, salt, vanilla and egg whites.

Drop spoon-full of the mixture on your lined baking tray and bake for 25-30 minutes until they are golden brown.

Once they are cooled, dip them in the melted chocolate one by one and refrigerate them for 20-30 minutes.

12) After Dinner Mint Macarons

The inspiration for this recipe came from mint flavored chocolate which is unique in its taste and a favorite of many. There is something about mint chocolate which just satisfies those taste buds like nothing else. The nice minty taste can make it a great after dinner dessert.

Cooking Time: 120 Min

Makes: 20-25

List of Ingredients:

- 2 tbs. of any heavy whipping cream
- 100 g Egg whites
- Green Food coloring
- 1 Green and Black mint chocolate bar
- 90 g Almond meal
- 3.6 Tbs. Granulated sugar
- 181 g Powdered sugar
- 1 - teaspoons Real Vanilla extract

sssssssssssssssssssssssssssssssssssssssssssssssssss

Procedure:

Make basic French macarons and just add some green food color in your batter before baking to get that minty green look.

Break the chocolate into small pieces.

Microwave the cream for 10-15 seconds and then pour in the chocolate, allow it to sit for some minutes before you begin to sit.

Cool down the ganache before you pipe it into the macarons.

13) Chocolate Coconut Macaron

Chocolate coconut macarons may give you the look of a cookie but the texture and taste they have are more like of a candy bar. Moist and chewy you will for sure enjoy this satisfying taste with the dried coconut. The batter is extremely simple to make and the overall recipe does not take much time.

Cooking Time: 45 Min

Makes: 10

List of Ingredients:

- 3 large egg whites
- 4 ounces of semi-sweet or bittersweet chocolate, chopped
- ¼ cup of unsweetened cocoa powder, sifted
- 220g of sweetened flaked dried coconut
- ¼ teaspoon of salt
- ¾ cup of granulated white sugar
- 1 teaspoon of pure vanilla extract

sssssssssssssssssssssssssssssssssssssssssssssssssss

Procedure:

Take a double boiler and melt the chocolate and then set it aside to cool.

Now in a large bowl whisk your egg-whites, add in the cocoa powder, salt, sugar and vanilla extract and mix everything up.

Then stir in the coconut and melted chocolate thoroughly. Refrigerate to settle it down.

Pre-heat your oven to 325F and set your baking tray. Place mounds of the mixture and bake for 10-15 minutes.

14) Hazelnut Macaron with chocolate Frangelico ganache

If you are not a huge fan of what the typical almond flavor macarons have to offer, then these hazelnut macarons are perfect for you. Though they use almond flour like any other macarons but the taste of hazelnut is stronger.

Cooking Time: 120 Min

Makes: 20-25

List of Ingredients:

- 150 grams of sifted ground blanched hazelnuts
- 150 grams of sifter almond meal
- 300 grams of sifted powdered sugar
- 110 grams egg whites
- 300 grams white sugar
- 75 grams water
- 110 grams egg whites
- 8 oz. of good quality dark chocolate chopped into small chunks
- 1 cup of heavy cream
- 3 tbs. of Frangelico Hazelnut Liqueur

sssssssssssssssssssssssssssssssssssssssssssssssssss

Procedure:

Make the regular batter for the macarons but just add in the grounded blanched hazelnuts along with the almond meal.

Bake the cookies and let them cool down until we work on the filling.

Put the chopped chocolate in a large bowl and heat your cream until it starts to bubble and then stir in the Frangelico.

Pour the cream mixture into the chocolate and stir until it melts and the filling it smooth and creamy.

Once it cools down it will be perfect to fill in those baked macarons.

15) Almond Lemon Macarons

If you don't like coconut macarons, whether it's because of the chewy texture or the fat, this new macaroon recipe is something all cookie lovers will love. This is our crunchy alternative, macaron made with almonds. These are full of protein so you know you are not putting your health at risk.

Cooking Time: 45 Min

Makes: 10

List of Ingredients:

- Half cup of sugar
- 2 cups of un-blanched almonds
- 1 teaspoon extract of almond
- ½ teaspoon fresh lemon rind (grated)
- Pinch of salt
- 3 egg whites

sssssssssssssssssssssssssssssssssssssssssssssssssss

Procedure:

Preheat your oven to around 350 degree F.

Grind your almonds and pour them in a bowl.

Mix the sugar in, salt, lemon rind, and add some almond extract.

Move on to add and mix the egg whites.

Now with the help of spoon place one ball on the set baking tray.

Bake for around 15-20 minutes.

16) Clementine Macarons

Clementine's make their way in the winter season and have the perfect citrusy and tangy taste. These macarons are super tasty and have a fresh and fruity feel to them. The fruity taste balances out with the macaron cookie and both go along well.

Cooking Time: 120 Min

Makes: 20-25

List of Ingredients:

- 66g of egg whites
- 60g of caster sugar
- 100g unsalted butter
- 90g of almond flour
- 2g egg white powder
- 110g icing sugar
- 1/3 teaspoon clementine zest (grated)
- 250g icing sugar
- Some drops of orange food coloring
- 2 teaspoons lemon juice
- 2 tablespoons orange-infused milk (set aside a tablespoon of orange zest in about 2 tablespoons of milk to cool over the night)
- 3 teaspoons orange juice
- 2/3 teaspoon grated orange zest

sssssssssssssssssssssssssssssssssssssssssssssssssss

Procedure:

Make the regular batter for the macarons but just add in the zest and few drop of orange coloring to get the taste and look. Bake them and put them aside to cool down.

For the filling, beat the icing sugar and butter until creamy.

Now add in the zest and juice.

Add in the milk and beat until it becomes a mixture.

Fill the baked macarons with this cream and enjoy.

17) Strawberry and Vanilla Macaron trifle

Macarons are quite a favorite dessert of many people and an equal competitor is the trifle, for which everyone has their own recipe they love. So what happens when we combine both with the added taste of vanilla and strawberries? That's the recipe which we are just going to share with you!

Cooking Time: 20 Min

Makes: 10

List of Ingredients:

- 1 tbs. of vanilla extract
- 16 plain macarons
- 500ml of whipped cream
- 750ml of cranberry juice
- 700g of strawberries
- 110g of caster sugar

ssssssssssssssssssssssssssssssssssssssssssssssssssssss

Procedure:

First we will create the strawberry jelly for which we will add the gelatin and half cup of cranberry juice into a bowl and mix well. Set aside until the gelatin gets absorbed.

Put the remaining sugar and cranberry juice in a pan over heat and mix to the point the sugar is absorbed. Bring it to boil and then cook for a minute. Remove it from heat and add in the gelatin and stir so it gets combined. Cool it.

Now set the strawberries at the bottom of the bowl and then set the mixture of jelly on top of it. Refrigerate it for an hour or so. Now put the macarons on top of it. Fold in the vanilla extract inside the cream and create a layer over the macaron. Again top it off with strawberry.

18) Sunflower Seed Macarons with Black Truffle Salted White Chocolate

Sunflower seeds are very rich in nutrients and impart a nutty flavor to the shells of macarons. When you toast and ground them they are almost the same as grounded almond meal. This nutty aromatic recipe is perfect for all the macaron lovers.

Cooking Time: 120 Min

Makes: 20-25

List of Ingredients:

- 50g of egg white
- 1.5g of egg white powder
- 45g of caster sugar
- 75g of sunflower seeds
- 80g of icing sugar
- 70g of White chocolate
- 40ml of double cream
- 1/3 teaspoon of salt
- 1.5 teaspoon of chopped black truffles

ssssssssssssssssssssssssssssssssssssssssssssssssssssssss

Procedure:

Pre-heat your oven to 150 degrees C. Roast the sunflower seeds on a tray lined with aluminum for around 10 minutes and cool it down. Reduce the heat to 140 degree.

Now blitz the seeds and icing sugar in a processor to a grounded mixture. Sift the mixture into a bowl. Don't over-do this else oil will start to emerge which will make your macarons clumpy.

Take a separate bowl and whisk the egg whites and powder until peaks are formed. Then whisk in the caster sugar. Now fold in the dry mixture from the above step until a smooth paste is formed.

Now pipe this mixture and bake the shells of macarons.

For the filling take the white chocolate and cream in a double broiler and heat over simmering water until it melts down. Stir along as it melts.

Cool the mixture slightly and then add in the black truffles and salt. Refrigerate it until it sets before you fill them in the macarons.

19) Pumpkin Salted Caramel Butter Cream Macarons

Another treat for the pumpkin lovers! Perfect for any event on Halloween, this pumpkin recipe is created with salted caramel and butter cream. The salty taste is balanced out with the butter cream and on the whole it's as tasty as any other macaron can get.

Cooking Time: 120 Min

Makes: 25

List of Ingredients:

- 300g of powdered sugar
- 220g of egg whites
- 300g of almond meal
- 75g of water
- ¼ teaspoon flaky sea salt, crushed into fine powder
- 300g of granulated sugar
- 1 - teaspoons of pumpkin pie spice
- 8 ounces of European style butter at room temperature

- Half cup of sifted powdered sugar
- 16 ounces of caramel
- Half teaspoon of vanilla extract

sssssssssssssssssssssssssssssssssssssssssssssssssss

Procedure:

Add around 110g of egg whites in the almond and sugar mixture.

Boil some water and the granulated sugar till 115 degree C.

Start whipping the remaining of egg whites and pour the sugar mixture in it gradually until it cools down.

Now fold in the almond mixture into it.

Take a small bowl and mix some food color (light caramel) and the pumpkin spice with few spoons of the mixture created above and then add it to the mixture and blend in well.

Now pipe this mixture into small diameters on a lined baking tray.

Keep them at room temperature for an hour so the top becomes stiff.

Bake the macarons for 15-20 minutes in a pre-heated oven at 280 degrees F.

Whisk the butter in a bowl till creamy and then add the caramel and beat adding in the sugar and vanilla until everything it incorporated well.

Fold in the salt with the help of a spatula.

Refrigerate and then fill in the macaroons.

20) Dark Chocolate + Peanut Butter Banana Macarons

For all the peanut butter and chocolate lovers out there, these macarons are just for you. This is our personal favorite recipe as the taste never fails anyone. Peanut butter and chocolate, is there a combination which can get better then this?

Cooking Time: 120 Min

Makes: 20-25

List of Ingredients:

- 8 ounces of confectioner's sugar
- 4 ounces of almond flour
- 2 ½ ounces of granulated sugar
- A pinch salt
- Some yellow gel food coloring
- ½ cup of Dark Chocolate
- 5 ounces of egg whites
- Banana Peanut Butter
- 1 cup of confectioner's sugar
- ½ teaspoon of vanilla extract
- ¼ cup of softened unsalted butter
- 1 tablespoon of milk
- Pink salt

sssssssssssssssssssssssssssssssssssssssssssssssssssss

Procedure:

Make the regular macrons with just adding a pinch of yellow gel color to complete the look.

Bake them and set them aside to cool.

Now take the dark chocolate and peanut butter and mix them well.

Then add the butter, sugar, vanilla extract, milk and salt to taste to complete the filling.

Fill your macarons and enjoy.

21) Pumpkin Macarons

Looking for a Halloween treat? Well then you've just come across the perfect recipe! Till now you must have seen many recipes cooked from pumpkins but pumpkin macarons will not only be new to you but to those who you serve too! It's tasty, it's crunchy and it will melt into your mouth.

Cooking Time: 120 Min

Makes: 25

List of Ingredients:

- 300g of powdered sugar
- 220g of egg whites
- 300g of almond meal
- 75g of water
- 8 ounces of white chocolate
- 3 tbs. of heavy cream
- 300g of granulated sugar
- 2 tbs. of brown sugar
- 1 - teaspoons of pumpkin pie spice
- Half cup of canned pumpkin

sssssssssssssssssssssssssssssssssssssssssssssssssss

Procedure:

Add around 110g of egg whites in the almond and sugar mixture.

Boil some water and the granulated sugar till 115 degree C.

Start whipping the remaining of egg whites and pour the sugar mixture in it gradually until it cools down.

Now fold in the almond mixture into it.

Take a small bowl and mix some food color (light orange) with few spoons of the mixture created above and then add it to the mixture and blend in well.

Now pipe this mixture into small diameters on a lined baking tray.

Keep them at room temperature for an hour so the top becomes stiff.

Bake the macarons for 15-20 minutes in a pre-heated oven at 280 degrees F.

Melt the chocolate in a double boiler and set it aside.

Now add the cream, brown sugar, pumpkin spice, pumpkin in a small pan and bring it to simmer over low heat.

Add this mixture into the melted chocolate and set it first in fridge before you fill your macarons.

22) French Macaron Milkshake

Got some broken down macarons which you can't present to someone? Well not to worry because this recipe is perfect for all those left out macarons and is real quick to make too. A milkshake made from macarons, yes you heard us right!

Cooking Time: 15 Min

Makes: 2-3

List of Ingredients:

- 4 cups of vanilla ice cream
- 6-8 macarons
- Whipped cream

sssssssssssssssssssssssssssssssssssssssssssssssssssssss

Procedure:

Put the milk, ice cream and macarons in a blender and blend until smooth. Add some more milk if needed.

Pour it into glasses and garnish with whipped cream and macarons.

23) Peach Macarons

Peaches are quite a rich fruit. They're sweet, tangy and just fill your mouth with juicy freshness. So we decided to take this and add it up in tasty macarons which will take your taste buds on a savory ride. If you don't have peaches you can make the same recipe with some raspberries too. It's your personal choice.

Cooking Time: 120 Min

Makes: 20

List of Ingredients:

- 300g of powdered sugar
- 300g of almond meal
- 110g of egg whites
- ¼ peach preserves
- 75g of water
- 110g of egg whites
- 300g of granulated sugar
- 15 drops of peach essence
- Half cup of heavy cream
- 1 tablespoon of butter
- 16 ounces of white chocolate
- Half cup strained peach preserves

sssssssssssssssssssssssssssssssssssssssssssssssss

Procedure:

Add around 110g of egg whites in the almond and sugar mixture.

Boil some water and the granulated sugar till 115 degree C.

Start whipping the remaining of egg whites and pour the sugar mixture in it gradually until it cools down.

Now fold in the almond mixture into it.

Take a small bowl and mix some orange food color and 5 drops of peach essence with few spoons of the mixture created above and then add it to the mixture and blend in well.

Now pipe this mixture into small diameters on a lined baking tray.

Keep them at room temperature for an hour so the top becomes stiff.

Bake the macarons for 15-20 minutes in a pre-heated oven at 280 degrees F.

For the ganache, melt the chocolate over a double boiler.

Heat the cream, butter and strained preserves. Once melted add this into the chocolate and mix until it's blended nicely. Add in the remaining peach preserves and essence and whisk.

Cool it down and fill your macarons.

24) Lemon Blueberry Macaron Trifles

You can swap in any fruit of your choice or even mix different fruits to develop your own taste depending on the macarons you choose but this lemon and blueberry macaron trifle is just tasty as any other dessert out there! There is so much you can do with macarons and this recipe is proof of it.

Cooking Time: 15 Min

Makes: 4

List of Ingredients:

- Half to ¾ cups of mascarpone cheese
- 2 cups of sweetened whipped cream
- Zest (finely grated) of a fresh lemon
- 2 cups of blueberries
- 24 macaron cookies

sssssssssssssssssssssssssssssssssssssssssssssssssssssss

Procedure:

Mix a cup of the whipped cream into the cheese to lighten.

Fold in the remaining cream and then add the zest.

Half down the macarons if required.

Layer the macaron, cream and berries (or any other fruit) in dessert glasses and refrigerate for 2-3 hours before serving.

25) Peanut Butter and Jelly Macarons

This recipe is for those who can't even think of parting with peanut butter and jam, even we can't. This duo sandwich is now available in yummy macarons, so why not enjoy them for breakfast?

Cooking Time: 120 Min

Makes: 20

List of Ingredients:

- ½ cup of ground almonds
- 2 egg whites
- 1 ¼ cups of powdered sugar
- ¼ cup of ground peanuts
- 1/3 cup of granulated sugar
- 3 ounces white chocolate
- Half cup unsalted butter
- ¾ cup of powdered sugar
- Pinch of salt
- 2 tablespoons of strawberry jam

sssssssssssssssssssssssssssssssssssssssssssssssss

Procedure:

Follow the recipe of basic French macarons and create your batter with the addition ingredient of ground peanuts.

Bake the macarons and set them aside.

Now whip the butter with salt till it becomes fluffy. Then slowly add in the sugar along with melted white chocolate.

Keep on beating to incorporate everything.

Now add the jam and beat until it become fluffy and light.

Fill in the cookies and put it in fridge to cool down before serving.

26) Macaron Banana Splits

Love banana splits? Can't get enough of them? Well then give the traditional banana split a twist by adding some crushed macarons as sprinkles. Set out your favorite ones and make this delight more savory and see if you can resist it.

Cooking Time: 15 Min

Makes: 4

List of Ingredients:

- 8 small bananas, peeled
- ½ cup of chocolate sauce
- 2 pints of ice cream (any flavor of choice)
- 12 macaron cookies
- ½ cup of sweetened whipped cream
- Sprinkles, chopped nuts etc. for topping

ssssssssssssssssssssssssssssssssssssssssssssssssss

Procedure:

Slice your bananas in a way so they sit flat on a plate.

Top the bananas with ice-cream, whipped cream, chocolate sauce and crushed macarons.

27) Meyer Lemon Macarons

Meyer lemons are a mix of regular lemon and orange so expect a citrus-filled taste. Now add this hybrid with macarons and you'll get something so refreshing and tasty which will just leave you wanting more.

Cooking Time: 120 Min

Makes: 20

List of Ingredients:

- 200g of powdered sugar
- 110g of almond flour/meal
- 30g granulated sugar
- 3 aged egg whites (keep them covered at room temperature for 24 hours)
- Zest from 1 Meyer lemon
- 2 egg whites
- Yellow food coloring
- Half cup of sugar
- 1/8 teaspoon of cream of tartar
- ¼ teaspoon of salt
- 2 sticks unsalted butter
- 3 tablespoons of lemon juice
- ½ teaspoon of vanilla extract
- Zest of 1-2 lemons

sssssssssssssssssssssssssssssssssssssssssssssssss

Procedure:

Make you batter for macarons by adding the zest and yellow food coloring to complement the recipe.

Bake the macarons and set them aside.

Take a double boiler and add the egg whites, salt, sugar and tarter. Mix until it becomes warm. Remove it from the heat and take a whisker. Beat until it has stiff peaks.

Now add the butter slowly while beating continuously. Lastly add in the vanilla, juice and zest.

Set the mixture in a fridge before filling the macarons with it.

28) Lavender Macarons with honey buttercream

Lavenders are one of those flowers which are mostly used in cooking mainly because of their delicate fragrance and amazing color and the delicate taste they give to the recipes. So today we have this lavender and honey cream macaron recipe for you.

Cooking Time: 120 Min

Makes: 20

List of Ingredients:

- 1 cup of confectioners' sugar
- ¾ of cup almond meal
- 3 Tablespoons of sugar
- 2 egg whites
- ½ cup of butter
- 1 tablespoon of dried lavender buds
- 2 Tablespoons of honey
- 1 cup of confectioner's sugar

sssssssssssssssssssssssssssssssssssssssssssssssssssssss

Procedure:

Create the batter for the macarons by blending the lavender buds with the almond mixture. Bake the macarons and set them aside to cool off.

Now for the filling, beat the butter with a whisker for around 2-3 minutes and then slowly add in the sugar and whisk until everything is one.

Do the same with honey.

Fill your baked macarons with this filling and enjoy.

29) Eggnog Macarons

Due to the use of nutmeg in this recipe, it turns out be a bit spicy but in a sweet way. The spice is just the perfect amount so don't get overwhelmed by it. The taste of eggnog is not too overpowering and is overall a great recipe.

Cooking Time: 120 Min

Makes: 20

List of Ingredients:

- 90 grams of egg whites
- 110 grams of blanched almonds
- 25 grams of granulated sugar
- 2 egg whites
- 200 grams of powdered sugar
- Half cup of sugar
- ¾ - teaspoons of ground cinnamon
- 12 Tbs. butter
- Pinch of salt
- ¼ - teaspoons of nutmeg

sssssssssssssssssssssssssssssssssssssssssssssssss

Procedure:

Make your basic French macarons and set them aside.

For the filling, whisk the egg whites, sugar and salt in a bowl. Set this bowl over a small pan of boiling water and whish until the sugar is dissolved.

Remove it from the water and whisk the egg whites into soft peaks.

Now blend in the butter slowly and then increase the speed until the buttercream comes together.

Store it in a fridge for some time so it settles.

Then fill the macarons.

Sprinkle the macarons with some nutmeg powder.

30) Chocolate and Nutella Macarons

Who doesn't like Nutella? We think no one has the courage to make such a statement and this is why we have combined two favorite things, Nutella and macarons and came up with this amazing recipe. Something perfect to lift your mood on any gloomy day.

Cooking Time: 120 Min

Makes: 20

List of Ingredients:

- 200g of powdered sugar
- 110g of blanched slivered almonds
- 50g of granulated sugar
- 3 large egg white
- 2 Tbs. cocoa powder (dark or regular)
- ½ cup of heavy cream
- 3 Tbs. of Nutella
- 2 oz. of any bittersweet chocolate

ssssssssssssssssssssssssssssssssssssssssssssssssssssss

Procedure:

Mix the cocoa powder in the batter of macarons and bake them as regular French macarons.

Now come to the filling.

Place the Nutella and chocolate in a bowl.

Then bring the cream to simmer and pour it over the Nutella and let it sit for some seconds.

Mix until the mixture becomes smooth and creamy.

Place the mixture in the fridge so that it can settle.

Now fill your macaron cookies with it and enjoy.

About the Author

Allie Allen developed her passion for the culinary arts at the tender age of five when she would help her mother cook for their large family of 8. Even back then, her family knew this would be more than a hobby for the young Allie and when she graduated from high school, she applied to cooking school in London. It had always been a dream of the young chef to study with some of Europe's best and she made it happen by attending the Chef Academy of London.

After graduation, Allie decided to bring her skills back to North America and open up her own restaurant. After 10 successful years as head chef and owner, she decided to sell her business and pursue other career avenues. This monumental decision led Allie to her true calling, teaching. She also started to write e-books for her students to study at home for practice. She is now the proud author of several e-books and gives private and semi-private cooking lessons to a range of students at all levels of experience.

Stay tuned for more from this dynamic chef and teacher when she releases more informative e-books on cooking and baking in the near future. Her work is infused with stores and anecdotes you will love!

Author's Afterthoughts

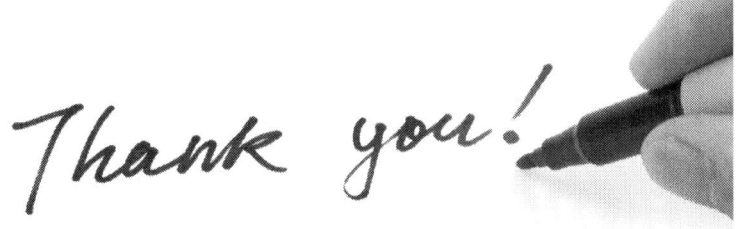

I can't tell you how grateful I am that you decided to read my book. My most heartfelt thanks that you took time out of your life to choose my work and I hope you find benefit within these pages.

There are so many books available today that offer similar content so that makes it even more humbling that you decided to buying mine.

Tell me what you thought! I am eager to hear your opinion and ideas on what you read as are others who are looking for a good book to buy. Leave a review on Amazon.com so others can benefit from your wisdom!

With much thanks,

Allie Allen

Printed in Great Britain
by Amazon